PLANET
EARTH

PLANET EARTH

CHRISTOPHER LAMPTON

FRANKLIN WATTS
NEW YORK/LONDON/TORONTO/SYDNEY/1982
A FIRST BOOK

Not AR

Cover photograph courtesy of NASA

Interior photographs courtesy of NASA: pp. ii, 20, 23, 28, 33, 35, 58; the American Museum of Natural History: p. 12; Vantage Art, Inc.: p. 24; United Press International: p. 27; NOAA: pp. 29, 43; American Airlines: p. 36; Carolina Biological Supply Co.: p. 52; Standard Oil Co. (N.J): p. 55; Los Angeles Zoo: p. 56; n.c.: p. 57.

Library of Congress Cataloging in Publication Data

Lampton, Christopher.
Planet earth.

(A First book)
Bibliography: p.
Includes index.
Summary: Describes the planet Earth as it exists today, explaining how it came into being and how it has evolved through the interplay of air, water, rock, and living things.
1. Earth—Juvenile literatures. [1. Earth. 2. Ecology] I. Title.
QB631.L27   550   81-21898
ISBN 0-531-04387-8   AACR2

CONTENTS

PLANET EARTH

CHAPTER ONE

A WORLD AMONG WORLDS

What is the earth?

On a clear night, you can stand in an open field and watch bright pinpoints of light pass overhead. These are the stars. As time passes, your view of these stars will change. New stars will rise over the eastern horizon and set in the west. Yet night after night, the stars themselves remain the same, or so nearly the same that your eyes will detect no difference. The North Star still shines above the Pole. The Milky Way still shimmers like a distant, jeweled veil. Year after year, we are treated to the same constellations—Orion the Hunter, the Big Dipper, Cygnus the Swan. For all practical purposes, the stars are constant and unchanging. Like beacons, they guide ships and airplanes and lost travelers through the trackless night.

And yet, the stars are not the only bright pinpoints of light in the sky. There are others that wander among these stars, seeming to pause briefly in this or that constellation, then moving on. These are the *planets.* Their very name comes from a Greek word meaning "wanderer." They are much smaller than stars. But they are also much closer to us, so they seem larger and brighter. They orbit in great loops around the sun (which is also a star, but a very nearby one), and they shine by reflected sunlight.

The earth is one such planet.

This may be hard to accept. The earth is where we live. It is a place of trees and mountains and cities, of rivers and clouds and rainstorms, of people and animals and insects, of blue skies and brown soil and green grass. It is a *world,* not a light in the sky.

And yet, each of those distant pinpoints of light is a world in its own right. Venus, for instance, is a forbidding sphere of scalding gases and poison clouds. Jupiter is a huge ball of ice, gas, and rock, battered by hurricanes larger than the human mind can imagine. Saturn has its spectacular rings that operate according to natural laws astronomers do not yet fully understand.

What makes the earth unique? What sets it apart from these other worlds? It isn't nearly as large as Jupiter or as small and hot as Mercury. It is neither as beautiful as Saturn, nor as remote and cold as Pluto. Is there anything about our planet that makes it special, that lets the earth stand out even amid our rich and varied solar system?

Before we can properly answer this question, we must first know some facts. We must take a closer look at the planet on which we live to see what the Planet Earth is like today and how it got that way.

CHAPTER TWO

THE SPINNING CLOUD

For thousands of years, men and women believed that the earth was at the center of the universe.

It's easy to see why. Anyone with eyes knew that the stars and planets rotated around the earth. Every night, they could see them whirl past overhead. Every day, they could see the sun rise in the east and set in the west. It was obvious that the earth was the center of a great deal of activity.

According to this view, common until about 400 years ago, the stars were set in a great sphere that surrounded the earth. The planets, the moon, and the sun were set in smaller spheres, inside the sphere that held the stars. At the center of all these spheres was the earth, around which everything else revolved.

In ancient Greece, however, there were a few astronomers who believed otherwise. Aristarchus of Samos, who lived more than 2,000 years ago, thought that the earth and the other planets revolved around the sun. This was hardly a popular opinion. Later, during the period known as the Dark Ages, it was considered blasphemous to suggest that the earth was not at the center of the universe. In the sixteenth century, the Polish astronomer Nicolaus Copernicus revived the theories of Aristarchus. But Copernicus wisely arranged that his views not be published until after his death. Giordano Bruno, an Italian philos-

opher, was burned at the stake in 1600 for preaching Copernicus's ideas.

Today we know that the earth is one of nine planets that orbit the sun. The sun itself is only one of billions of suns (or stars) that make up a vast spiral of stars that we call the *Milky Way*. And the Milky Way is only one of millions of similar collections of stars called *galaxies*.

This must have been a bitter pill for people to swallow. If the earth is only one of nine planets circling one of billions of stars, in one of millions of galaxies, how insignificant we are! How small we seem against the vastness of the universe!

And yet the earth *is* significant—to those of us who live on it. And even if space travel becomes more common in the years ahead, the earth is where most of will spend our lives, so we'd better understand it.

We cannot go back in time to watch the solar system form, but we can observe other stars, where planets may be forming right now. From such studies and from studies of the planets of the solar system as they are today, we can now make some good guesses about how the earth—and the rest of the solar system—was born.

Imagine a cloud of dust and gas floating in space, spinning in slow circles like a giant top. The gas and dust in the cloud are made up of tiny particles called *atoms*. (In fact, nearly everything in our universe is made up of atoms.) There are many different kinds of atoms in this cloud, each one representing a different element. Elements are the basic substances of the universe, from which all other substances are made, and each element is made up of a single kind of atom. Most of the atoms in this cloud represent the element hydrogen, the simplest (and

Nicolaus Copernicus, 1473–1543

—13

most common) element in the universe. However, there are many other elements in the cloud, in smaller amounts.

Each atom in the cloud possesses a property called *gravity*. Gravity causes the atoms to be attracted to one another. Because of this attraction, they begin to move closer together. As they do so, the cloud begins to shrink.

Several things happen as the cloud shrinks. Have you ever watched ice skaters spin on their skates? If so, you may have noticed that the skaters spin faster with their arms held tightly against their sides than extended at full length. The same thing happens with our cloud. As it shrinks (pulling in its "arms") it spins faster. And the more it shrinks, the faster it spins.

Also, as it shrinks and spins, the atoms in the cloud begin to run into one another. When two atoms collide, they create heat through a kind of friction, just as hot sparks can be created by striking two stones together. In the same way, our shrinking cloud becomes hot. It becomes so hot that all of the elements in the cloud—even elements that we normally think of as solid, like iron—turn into gases.

The cloud collapses into a spinning ball. The ball spins so rapidly that it begins to bulge around the middle. As the ball spins faster, the bulge grows larger, until the ball is shaped more like a disk, or saucer. At the center of this saucer is a lump of glowing matter. Because there are more atoms in this lump than in the disk, there are more collisions between atoms —and the lump becomes hotter than the rest of the cloud. Meanwhile, the thin outer edge of the saucer begins to cool. As it cools, some of the gases become solid matter again. They form into large chunks, circling around the outer part of the disk.

The process we are describing is the way in which our solar system was probably born, roughly 5 billion years ago. The chunks of solid matter will eventually come together to form the planets, including the earth. The lump at the center will become the sun.

Let's take a closer look at the chunks of matter that will become the earth. They are made up mostly of the elements iron and nickel, with some silicates (the substances from which rocks are made). These chunks of metal and rock frequently collide with one another. Occasionally, they stick together, forming larger chunks. Eventually, these larger chunks come together to form a single large chunk. Like the atoms of which it is made, the large chunk has gravity. The molecules of gas left over from the interstellar cloud (mostly hydrogen, helium, neon, methane, ammonia, and water vapor) are attracted to the chunk and surround it. We now have what scientists call a *protoplanet,* a planet that has not yet taken its final shape. This "protoearth" is 500 times as large as the earth is today.

You'll remember that the lump of matter at the center of the proto-solar system—the lump that will become the sun—is very hot, because of the friction of colliding atoms. When a certain temperature is reached in this lump, a new process begins. When two very hot hydrogen atoms run into one another, they fuse (join) together to form a larger atom. When this happens, a burst of energy is given off that shoots out into space in the form of light and heat. This process is called *hydrogen fusion.* It is the same process by which hydrogen bombs explode. This process changes the protosun into a real sun.

The tremendous heat of hydrogen fusion creates a kind of shock wave, or wind, that sweeps most of the gases out of the inner part of the solar system. The protoplanets lose their thick shells of gas, and nothing is left behind except the iron-nickel cores, some silicates, and a few of the heavier gases. Without their thick shells of gas, these planets actually become smaller than they are today. However, this early solar system is still filled with small particles of solid matter. The newly formed planets are bombarded by these particles. As these particles collect on their surfaces, the planets slowly grow in size.

This is how scientists think the earth formed. As chunks of rock and metal bombarded its surface, the earth grew hot.

(This heat is similar to that created by colliding atoms in the protosun.) For millions of years, the earth must have been hot and molten. Iron and nickel particles, being very heavy, would have sunk to the center of the molten earth. The rocky silicates, being lighter, would have floated near the surface.

Eventually, the bombardment of the earth slowed down, and the outer, rocky crust of the planet cooled.

The early earth had no oxygen. No human being could have survived long on its surface. There would have been nothing for her or him to breathe. Most of the atmosphere of this early earth came from *inside* the planet. Volcanoes released gases trapped inside the earth's molten interior. This process is called *outgassing*.

As the outer crust of the earth cooled, a long rain began. The rain must have lasted for millions of years, until most—but not all—of the water vapor in the atmosphere had turned into liquid water. This long rain filled the earth's oceans and rivers (though these early oceans did not much resemble the oceans of today).

There are scientists who believe that the earth passed through several significant turning points in its early history. The atmosphere of the primitive earth was different from the atmosphere we know today. It contained elements that would have trapped the sun's heat in such a way that the air would have become very hot, even after the molten inner earth had cooled to its present temperature. Because this is similar to the way heat becomes trapped in a greenhouse, we call this a *greenhouse effect*.

Because of this greenhouse effect, the average temperature of the earth's atmosphere would have slowly risen. If it had gone higher than about 125°F (51.6°C), we might have had what scientists call a *runaway greenhouse*—the temperature rise would have become irreversible. Our planet would have become a fiery inferno much like the planet Venus. Life as we know it could not have come into existence.

Fortunately, the earth's atmosphere changed with time (for reasons that we will discuss later). The greenhouse effect lessened, and the atmosphere cooled off. Catastrophe was narrowly averted.

However, the sun was cooler in those days than it is now. When the temperature began to go down, it might have kept on going down, until the earth was much colder than it is now. If the average atmospheric temperature had gone below about 41°F (5°C), the earth would have become a frozen snowball of a world. Snow and ice would have reflected most of the sun's heat back into space, and the cooling trend, like the earlier heating trend, would have become irreversible. Fortunately, our sun grew warmer in time to avert this second catastrophe.

How lucky we are! Long before the first human being walked the earth, our fate was decided. If the earth had been a little closer to the sun, and therefore slightly warmer, it would now be a fiery hell. If it had been a little farther away, and therefore slightly cooler, it would be an icy snowball. It has even been suggested that if the planet Jupiter had been only a little larger, its fierce gravity might have kept the protoearth from forming, and today our planet would be nothing more than a collection of loose rocks, like the asteroid belt.

But the earth did form, and so began a process of constant change that is still taking place today.

CHAPTER THREE

THE FORCES
THAT BUILD...

The earth that formed from the cooling protoplanet, some 4.6 billion years ago, was a lot like the earth we know today. Yet it was also very different.

For the first few hundred million years, our planet would have released its heat steadily into space. Its surface would have cooled, forming the earth's crust. Then, as savage volcanoes ripped holes through this crust, large amounts of heat would have been released from the planet's interior. Slowly, the earth would have reached its present temperature.

Yet even today the earth is far from cool. If you dug a hole in your backyard and burrowed straight downward, you would find that the temperature rose 1°F for every 60 feet (18 m) that you descended. Geologists tell us that much of the earth's core is made of liquid rock, at temperatures greater than 7,200°F (4,000°C).

Where does this heat come from? Is it left over from the days of the molten protoplanet? No. The earth would have lost its original heat in only a few million years.

The heat inside the earth is produced by certain elements. These elements are made up of highly unstable atoms. We call these atoms unstable because they sometimes change into other kinds of atoms. As they change, they release energy, much of it in the form of heat. Because this energy "radiates" outward from the atom in all directions, we call it *radiation*. Elements that produce radiation are referred to as *radioactive*.

Very little of this heat reaches the surface of the earth, where we live. (When it does, it is usually in the form of volcanic lava, geysers, or hot springs.) Most of the heat on the surface of the earth comes from the sun.

Yet this crust on which we live represents only the smallest fraction of our planet. We can compare the earth's crust to the skin of an apple. In proportion to the size of our planet, the earth's crust is almost exactly as thick as the apple's skin is compared to the size of the apple. Below that skin is a thick layer of extremely hot rock that we call the *mantle*. Temperatures in the mantle are very high. Ordinarily, such temperatures would be high enough to melt the mantle rock, turning it into molten liquid. But the mantle is squeezed tightly by the pressure of the rocks above. This pressure keeps the mantle so tight and compact that it cannot melt or turn into a liquid. Thus it remains solid.

And yet in some ways the mantle behaves as though it *were* a liquid. When earthquake waves pass through it, the mantle vibrates as though it were solid rock. Yet it moves around within the earth as though it were liquid. For this reason, we say that the mantle is *plastic*, or *semisolid*.

Such substances are not uncommon. Glass, for instance, normally behaves as though it were solid. But if you examine glass window panes from hundreds of years ago, you will find that they are thicker at the bottom than at the top. The glass has actually flowed downward, as though it were a thick syrup!

If the earth's crust is the skin of our imaginary apple, then the mantle is the pulp. It follows that the earth, like our apple, would have a core.

And so it does. In fact, it has two cores, one inside the other. Appropriately, these are called the *inner core* and the *outer core*.

The outer core is entirely liquid. We refer to this liquid as

magma. It is made mostly of iron and nickel. The inner core is made of the same elements, but it is solid, probably because of the extreme pressure created by the magma above it.

We saw a moment ago that the interior of the earth is constantly being heated by radioactive elements. We don't feel much of this heat on the surface of the earth, yet it does have an important effect on our lives.

The surface of the earth, to most of us who live on it, seems like a steady, unchanging place. Yet over the billions of years that the earth has existed, that surface has been in a constant state of change.

The key to the earth's changing surface lies at the bottom of the ocean. But no one even knew it existed until the discovery of the largest mountain range in the world—an underwater range that was first spotted by seagoing vessels shortly after World War II. Called the *Mid-Ocean Ridge*, the range stretches for more than 45,000 miles (72,000 km)—around the entire world, in fact. Some of the ridge's peaks are more than 10,000 feet (3,000 m) high; many of them stick up out of the ocean, where they appear as islands. Some of these peaks are volcanic.

The Mid-Atlantic Ridge, which is the Atlantic portion of the Mid-Ocean Ridge, extends for nearly 25,000 miles (40,000 km). At its center is a rift, or valley, containing a series of holes or vents that extend down into the earth. Water that flows into these holes comes back hot, as though it had passed through some kind of heating system beneath the ocean floor.

This heating system, scientists believe, is the reason for

Lake Titicaca
in the Andes Mountains
in South America

the ridge's existence. Hot lava rises up into the rift from within the earth, just as hot air rises over a fire. When it touches the cooler water, it hardens into rock—and forms the mountains of the ridge.

The lava rising up from the rift is made up of the plastic substance of the mantle. Because the mantle is semisolid, it rises very slowly, over millions of years. However, as this hot, plastic material nears the surface, the pressure of the overlying rock decreases. The hot mantle, no longer squeezed by this pressure, is free to melt. It emerges into the ocean as molten lava and solidifies into the material that makes up the ridge.

The rising of the mantle causes the ocean floor to bulge. Over millions of years, gravity pulls the ocean floor down the sides of this bulge, away from the middle section of the rift. This pulls the rift apart, widening the holes at its center. More lava flows up from below to fill these holes and to build new mountains along the sides of the rift. Thus the rift never actually becomes wider.

In this way, new ocean floor is constantly being created. The Atlantic Ocean, as a result of the lava rising at its center, is becoming wider at a rate of 2 to 10 centimeters per year. The expanding ocean floor, in turn, presses against the continents on both sides of the ocean. This pushes them away from one another.

If Europe and America are drifting apart, we might guess that they were once closer together, perhaps even part of the same continent. This is true. In fact, 200 million years ago all of the continents of the world—North and South America, Europe, Asia, Africa, Australia, and Antarctica—were a single, giant continent. Geologists call this supercontinent *Pangaea* (from

India and Ceylon,
part of the modern day
continent of Asia

—22

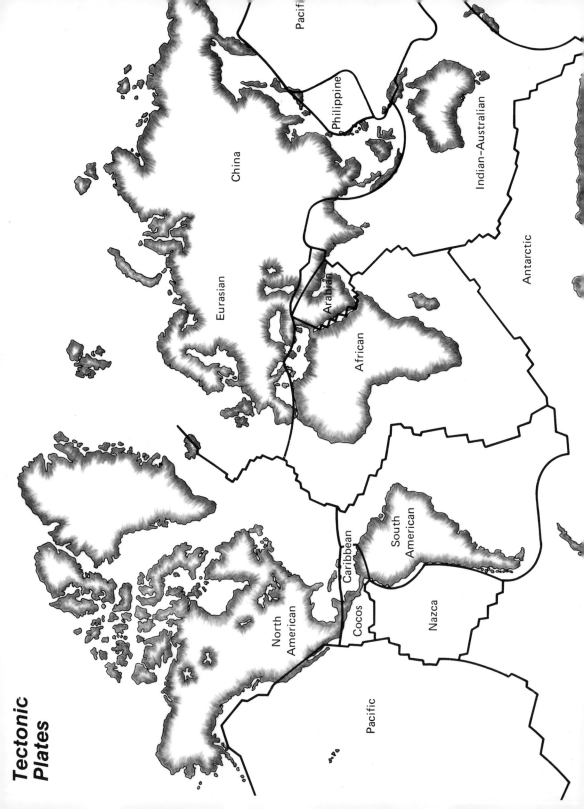

Tectonic Plates

Greek words meaning "all lands"). Pangaea floated in the middle of a giant ocean called *Panthalassa* ("all oceans").

Eventually, heat pressure from inside the earth broke up the supercontinent of Pangaea. At first, it drifted apart into two smaller continents, one to the north and one to the south. (We call the northern continent *Laurasia* and the southern continent *Gondwanaland.*) These continents then broke up to form the continents we know today.

The continents and the ocean bottoms rest on bodies that scientists call *plates.* These are made from a combination of crust and mantle materials. They float on the semisolid mantle in much the same way a raft floats on water. The heat from inside the earth keeps these plates in constant motion. The study of that motion is called *plate tectonics.*

New plate material is constantly being created all along the Mid-Ocean Ridge. If new plate material is being created, what happens to the old plate material? Is the earth growing larger, to make room for the increased surface area? There is no evidence for this, so there must also be places where old plate material is being destroyed.

Such places are called *subduction zones.* At a subduction zone, one plate actually rides over another. The lower plate sinks into the earth, where it melts and becomes part of the mantle.

Sometimes, the sinking plate will scrape material from the overriding plate. This material will be carried down into the mantle. When it melts, however, it will rise up underneath the overriding plate. As it presses against the plate, the crust of the earth will actually rise at that point, and mountains or plateaus will form. Volcanoes may occur in these regions if the molten material breaks through the crust. A subduction zone may be responsible for the so-called Ring of Fire, a region encircling the Pacific Ocean where volcanic activity is unusually common. The Mount St. Helens volcano in Washington State is part of this ring.

Mountains may also form where two plates collide. Less than a hundred million years ago, the subcontinent of India collided with Southcentral Asia. The land buckled at the point of collision, just as the hood of a car might buckle during a collision with another car. This buckling resulted in the Himalaya Mountains, which contain some of the highest peaks in the world today, including Mount Everest.

Sometimes volcanoes will appear in the middle of plates. Apparently these are caused by "hot spots" in the mantle. As the plates move across these areas of rising magma, lava occasionally erupts through the crust. The volcanic islands of the Pacific, including the Hawaiian chain, were probably caused by such hot spots. If you look at a map, you will see that these islands appear in long strings, a result of the slow northwestward movement of the Pacific plate across the hot spots.

In California there is a long flaw in the earth's crust called the San Andreas Fault. This is the point at which the North American plate meets the Pacific plate. The two plates move sideways against one another along the fault. This sliding movement is not a steady one. Friction often causes the plates to stick. Forces build up inside the earth, trying to overcome this friction. When the forces are strong enough, the plates begin to move again, but this movement can be sudden and violent. The result is an earthquake. The tremors that radiate outward from the fault can destroy property and take lives. They can also change the shape of the land, even raising hills and mountains as the plates shift abruptly in relation to one another.

The Mount St. Helens
eruption of
May 18, 1980.

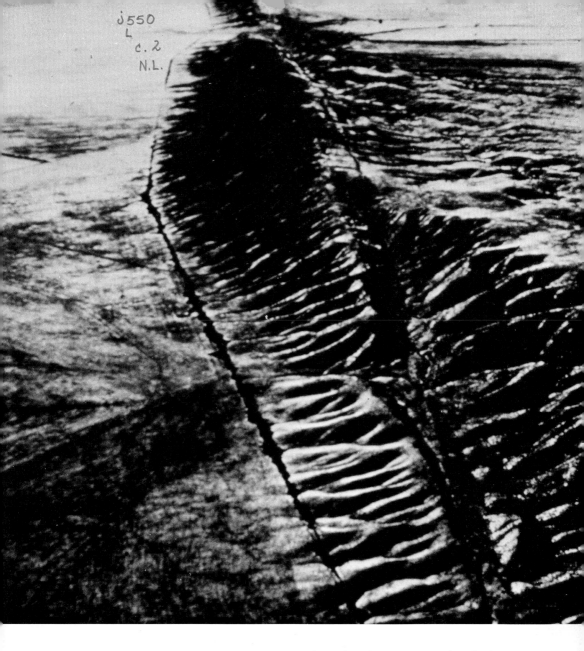

Opposite: *the Himalaya mountain chain*
Above: *the San Andreas Fault*

In this chapter, we have seen several forces that change the shape of the earth's surface. Some of these forces are so powerful that they can create mountains.

Mountain formation has gone on for most of the earth's 4.6-billion-year history. Yet even the oldest mountains on earth today are fairly young in geologic terms.The Appalachians, located in eastern North America, were probably formed when the continental plates came together to form Pangaea. They are only a few hundred million years old. This is a short time, compared to the age of the earth itself. Yet few mountains are older.

If there are forces that raise mountains, then there must be forces that wear them down. We'll take a look at some of these in the next chapter.

CHAPTER FOUR

...AND THE FORCES THAT DESTROY

The earth is surrounded by a shell of gases called the *atmosphere.* It is difficult to say just how thick this shell is. As we move upward from the earth's surface, the atmosphere becomes thinner and thinner. At some point, this thinning atmosphere blends into the near-perfect vacuum of outer space. (Even so-called empty space contains a few atoms of gas.)

As we saw in the first chapter, the earth's atmosphere was released from rocks inside the planet, mostly through volcanoes. This atmosphere has changed over time. Today, the chief gases in the atmosphere are nitrogen and oxygen, with small amounts of other gases, including carbon dioxide.

This atmosphere is important to living creatures. Not only does it provide us with the air that we breathe, but it also helps to distribute heat.

If you've ever left your house without a jacket on a cold day, you know how important heat is to living creatures. Most of the heat on the surface of the earth comes from the sun. When we stand outside on a summer afternoon, we can feel this heat pouring over us. The sunlight touches our skin, and our skin becomes warm. If we go indoors, however, this heat seems to follow us, even though the sunlight can no longer touch our skin. This is because the sun warms the air, and the air, in turn, keeps us warm, even indoors.

The spreading of heat through our atmosphere results in the process we call *weather.* Consider what happens, for instance, when warm air rises.

Usually, air contains a certain amount of water vapor, which enters the atmosphere from the oceans and other bodies of water through the process of evaporation. As the warm air rises, it becomes cooler. (The temperature of the atmosphere decreases with height, at least for the first 10 to 20 miles, or 16 to 32 km, above the ground.) Cold air cannot hold as much water vapor as warm air, so the water leaves the air and forms tiny droplets, which group together into clouds. Thousands of these cloud droplets can then join together to form larger droplets. The result is rain. If the temperature is low, the result may instead be snow.

As this warm air rises above the ground, more air is forced to rush in and take its place. This sideways motion of air is what we call *wind.*

Warm air tends to rise. Cold air tends to fall. Warm, rising air is lighter in weight than cold, falling air. We refer to an area where air is rising as a *low-pressure area* because the warm air puts less pressure on the ground than the cold air does. Similarly, we refer to an area where air is falling as a *high-pressure area* because the heavy, cold air places more pressure on the ground. Weather forecasters use a device called a barometer to measure air pressure. You might think of a barometer as a device for weighing air.

Why is it important to know what the air pressure is? Well, when the air pressure is low, the air will tend to rise. Rising air leads to rain and other kinds of storms. Therefore, storms will usually occur in low-pressure areas. On the other hand, rain almost never occurs in falling air. Therefore, in a high-pressure area, the weather is usually calm and clear. If you know the air pressure, then you can usually predict the weather.

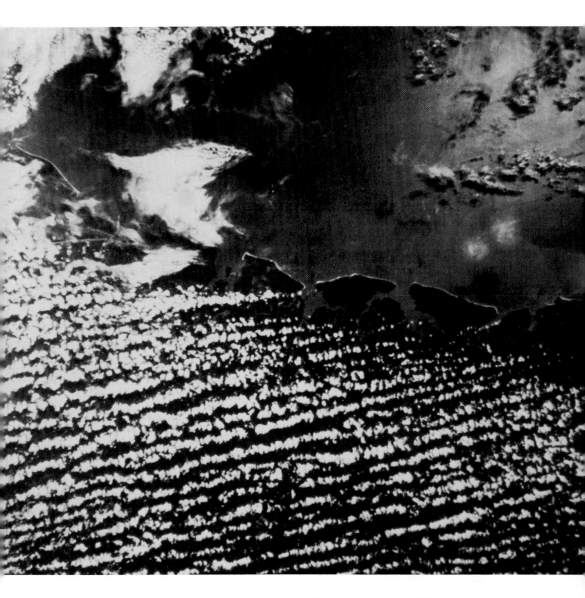

*Clouds over the U.S. east coast,
highlighted by the sun*

In parts of the world where the weather is very cold or very hot over large areas, such as at the North Pole or in the tropics, masses of air can form that are the same temperature throughout. Such an *air mass* can then move from its *source region* (the area where it forms) to other parts of the world. When two air masses of different temperatures bump into one another, they do not mix together. Rather, they act like two cars colliding. They flatten out at the point where they touch. The line between the two is called a *front*. One air mass usually ends up pushing the other air mass. When a warm air mass pushes a cold air mass ahead of it, we call it a *warm front*. When a cold air mass pushes a warm air mass ahead of it, we call it a *cold front*. In either case, the lighter, warmer air will run over the top of the heavier, colder air. This causes the warm air to rise. Just as rising air in a low-pressure area leads to rain, so the rising air in the warm air mass will create storms. Warm fronts and cold fronts are usually associated with rain and other storms. Because the air rises faster around a cold front than around a warm front, the most violent storms are often associated with cold fronts.

Because more sunlight falls on the equator than anywhere else on earth, the air is warmer there. It tends to rise. Therefore, the equator is a place of rain and violent storms. The North and South Poles, by the opposite token, are places of very calm weather.

Weather has played a significant part in shaping the face of the earth. For instance, wind and rain are two of the forces that destroy the mountains we examined in the last chapter. These forces grind away at rocks, breaking them down into small pieces that are then carried away to the ocean. This process is called *erosion*.

When rain falls on exposed rocks, certain elements in the rain combine with certain elements in the rock, and gradually the rock begins to crumble. The wind sweeps away the crumbled pieces. These pieces might then be carried by rainwater to a river. The river might carry these pieces to the ocean.

A cyclonic storm as seen from above, over the Pacific Ocean near Hawaii.

These pieces of waterborne rock are called *sediment*. They are usually very small. They settle to the ocean (or river) bottom, and more sediment settles on top of them. Eventually, the weight of the overlying sediment squeezes the water out of these pieces, and they become cemented together to form new rock called *sedimentary rock.*

As the earth changes with time, pieces of this sedimentary rock sometimes return to the surface, only to find themselves eroded again into sediment. At other times, this rock may settle deep within the earth, where it is melted by high temperatures. If this molten rock should again reach the earth's surface, it will cool and harden into another kind of rock that we call *igneous rock* (from a Latin word meaning "fire").

Either igneous or sedimentary rock can be affected by extreme pressures and temperatures within the earth in such a way that it is transformed into a third kind of rock—*metamorphic rock* (from Greek words meaning "transformation"). Limestone, for instance, is sedimentary rock formed out of the eroded shells of prehistoric sea creatures. When limestone is subjected to extreme pressures and high temperatures, it changes into marble, a metamorphic rock.

These, then, are the three types of rock—igneous, sedimentary, and metamorphic. It is not uncommon for one type of rock to change, under the right circumstances, into another type. Geologists call this the *rock cycle.*

Rivers have a powerful effect on the landscape. Not only do they provide channels in which sediment can travel, they also carve out deep grooves in the earth's surface. These grooves can become great canyons if they are cut deeply enough. The

*The Grand Canyon
and Colorado River*

Grand Canyon, in Arizona, is an excellent example of such a groove, etched into the desert by the Colorado River.

Changes in temperature can also contribute to erosion. When rock is heated, it expands. When it cools, it shrinks. If temperature changes occur unevenly throughout the rock, cracks will form. The rock will eventually crumble and be washed away to form sediment.

Frozen water also serves as an agent of erosion, though it works at a much slower pace than liquid water. There have been periods in the earth's history when much of the planet's surface has been covered with great rivers of ice called *glaciers*. These periods are called *ice ages*.

No one is entirely sure what causes an ice age, but there are many theories. One theory says that, because the earth's position relative to the sun changes over thousands of years, the way in which our atmosphere receives heat also changes. Sometimes, it changes in such a way that large quantities of snow will fall over wide areas. This snow, being bright white in color, reflects most of the sun's heat directly back into space. Long periods of cold weather might result.

During an ice age, glaciers move slowly across the surface of the continents. They leave great scars on the land, picking up sediment as they travel. When the ice age ends and the glaciers melt, the sediment is deposited in their wake.

Thus, on the surface of the earth, continents move, the oceans grow and shrink, and mountains rise and fall.

But the oceans themselves contribute greatly to the shaping of the earth. We'll take a closer look at how in the next chapter.

CHAPTER FIVE

THE ETERNAL OCEAN

One of the things that sets the earth apart from the other planets of the solar system is water—330 million cubic miles of it. Nearly three fourths of the earth's surface is covered with water, most of it in the ocean.

We often speak of the earth as having five oceans—the Atlantic, the Pacific, the Indian, the Arctic, and the Antarctic. However, this isn't strictly true. All of these oceans are interconnected, so it's just as accurate to speak of the earth as having one large ocean—a world ocean—in which all the continents are really just islands.

Why should there be oceans at all? In the first chapter we saw how water and various gases were released from molten rock as the newborn earth cooled. For there to be oceans, however, the water had to settle into basins, the way bathwater settles into a tub. Where did these basins come from?

The earth's surface is made up mostly of granitic and basaltic rock. The granitic rocks are found mostly in the continents, the basaltic in the ocean basins. Because the granitic rocks are relatively light, they ride high on the plastic mantle, the way a wooden boat rides high on the waves. The heavier, basaltic rocks sink into the mantle, much as a stone sinks into the water. Therefore, the ocean basins are lower than the continents. And water, which tends to seek the lowest level, automatically fills the basins.

If there were no water on earth, the continents would appear as vast plateaus, the ocean basins as low valleys spotted with mountains. (In fact, there are features very much like this on the planet Venus, where the atmosphere is too hot for water to exist in liquid form.) Surprisingly, the continents do not end where the ocean begins. In most places the land slopes away gradually underwater, sometimes stretching downward for miles before it connects with the basaltic ocean bottom. This underwater incline is called the *continental shelf*.

When the edge of a continent borders on a subduction zone (see p. 25), there is often a sudden drop-off at the end of the continental shelf, with the ocean bottom plunging downward for miles. Such a drop is called a *trench*. These trenches are the deepest places in the ocean. They do not occur in the middle of the ocean, as you might expect, but always at the edge of a continental shelf. The deepest trench measured to date is the so-called Mariana Trench, near Guam. It is more than 35,000 feet (10,500 m) deep.

Until the 1940s it was generally believed that the ocean bottom was featureless, a flat plain stretching from continent to continent. There are a few places in the ocean that match this description. They are called *abyssal plains*. In general, however, the terrain on the ocean bottom is much more dramatic than anything found on dry land. This is because the forces of erosion, which slowly wear away mountains on the continents, are much weaker in the ocean, where the terrain is not exposed to wind and rain. There are mountains in the ocean higher than Mount Everest, valleys deeper than the Grand Canyon. The Hawaiian Islands, for instance, are undersea mountains tens of thousands of feet tall, so immense that they break through the surface of the ocean to form an *archipelago* (chain of islands).

—40

The sea is always in motion, its surface creased with ripples and waves. Anyone who has ever been to the shore knows what a wave is. The average wave seems to begin as a barely visible ripple rolling in from the ocean, then grows in size until it breaks on the beach in a burst of white foam.

Where do waves come from? How do they form?

Most waves are created by wind. As the wind blows across the ocean, it stirs the water, creating a pattern of motion that travels across the ocean's surface. This pattern is the wave. The size and strength of the wave is the result of three things —the speed of the wind, how long it blows, and the distance over which it blows. (The distance over which the wind blows is called its *fetch*.) If the wind is fast, if it blows for a long time, and if it has a long fetch, the waves will be large and powerful. Sailors at sea have reported seeing waves more than 100 feet (30 m) high.

Just as the wind and rain shape the continents that we live on, so these waves shape the seashore. As waves roll up the continental slope, they begin to "feel bottom." The water becomes shallower, and the waves become unstable. They fall forward and break. The water in these waves races onto the shore at high speeds.

There is a great deal of power in these waves, especially when they have been created during a storm, when high winds blow for long periods of time with a particularly long fetch. Storm-driven waves have been known to lift objects weighing many thousands of tons and move them great distances inland.

During a particularly violent storm, when very strong winds are present, waves can actually pile up one on top of another, creating a super wave known as a *storm surge.* These giant waves are extremely destructive. A storm surge that struck Galveston, Texas, in 1900 took more than 5,000 lives. Fortunately, modern weather forecasting techniques can tell us when one of these surges is likely to occur, so that such disasters can now usually be prevented. However, it is always a good idea to stay away from the seashore when a violent storm, such as a hurricane, is predicted.

Even ordinary waves have a dramatic effect on the shore. They can take rocks and slowly grind them into sand. (In fact, this is how beaches are formed.) Then, because the waves usually strike the shore at an angle, they can lift this sand and carry it for miles along the coast. In this way, entire beaches can be washed away overnight and deposited several miles away.

Another kind of wave is that created by a volcano or an earthquake. Such waves are generally larger than those created by wind, often catastrophically so. Sometimes incorrectly called tidal waves (they have nothing to do with tides), these waves are known to scientists as *tsunamis,* the Japanese name for them.

The most famous tsunami in recorded history took place after the underwater explosions of the volcano Krakatoa in late August 1883, in the East Indies (now Indonesia). It swept over entire islands, drowning more than 36,000 people.

Ironically, the warning sign that a tsunami is on the way is a sudden lowering of the water level. This is the low part of the wave, or *trough.* Minutes later the high part of the wave, or *crest,* flows in. Unfortunately, the drop in water level often serves to attract curious bystanders, because it exposes portions of the seabed that were not previously visible. Such luckless curiosity seekers are likely to be drowned when the crest of the wave arrives. Experienced seashore dwellers know that a sudden drop in water level means that it's time to move to higher ground.

As we've seen, the motion of the sea is affected by wind, volcanoes, and earthquakes. It is also affected by the moon.

If you've had much experience with the ocean, you know that the water level rises and falls periodically, roughly twice a

Tsunamis, such as this one that struck Hawaii, are often deadly and destructive.

day in most places. This rising and falling motion is called the *tide*.

The tide is caused mostly by the gravitational pull of the moon. As the moon passes over the ocean, its gravity actually lifts the level of the seawater, causing the ocean to bulge. This bulge creates a wave that literally stretches halfway around the earth. The tide rises (in most places) twice a day, once when the moon is almost directly overhead and once when it is on the opposite side of the earth.

The ocean, then, helps to make the earth unique among the known planets. It chips away at the seashore, sculpting beaches as an artist sculpts stone.

There is something else, though, that makes the earth unique, something that has an even more profound effect on the face of our planet.

That something is *life*.

CHAPTER SIX

IN THE WITCHES' CAULDRON

There was no oxygen in the atmosphere of the primitive earth.

If there had been, life on earth would not now exist. This seems odd, since so many forms of life today (including human beings) need oxygen to survive.

Yet, to the first forms of life on this planet, oxygen would have been deadly poison.

The atmosphere of the primitive earth was very little like the air we know today. It was rich with chemicals that would be unbreathable and foul-smelling to human beings. Because there was no oxygen in the air, dangerous and powerful radiations from the sun were allowed to reach the earth's surface. (Today, the oxygen in the atmosphere acts as a shield against many of these radiations.)

It was in this witches' cauldron of deadly radiations and strange vapors that life was born.

Like nearly everything else in the universe, living creatures are made of atoms. These atoms link themselves together in long chains called *molecules.*

The main difference between the molecules that make up living creatures and the molecules that make up everything else is that living molecules tend to be longer. *Much* longer. Often, a single molecule will contain millions, even billions, of atoms. Furthermore, these molecules are not always simple, straight chains, like necklaces. Usually, they are twisted together into complicated shapes.

Because such molecules are found mostly in living organisms, they are called *organic molecules.* The most important organic molecules are the nucleic acids and the amino acids. The amino acids link together to form large molecules called *proteins.* One kind of protein is the *enzyme.* Enzymes are molecular machines. They rearrange the way other molecules fit together within living creatures.

The primitive ocean was full of molecules. Occasionally, bolts of lightning or the harsh rays of the sun would knock these molecules apart, combining the atoms together into new molecules. In this way, different kinds of molecules were constantly forming in the primitive ocean. Some of these molecules were organic.

At what point did life begin? Organic molecules are the stuff of life, but they themselves are not alive. Many scientists believe that life began when, by random chance, a molecule formed that could make copies of itself.

Your body (and the bodies of other living organisms) is made up mostly of organic molecules. These molecules group together into structures we call *cells.* If the atom is the basic building block of matter, then the cell is the basic building block of life.

Each cell is a hive of chemical activity. This activity makes us what we are. Yet the cell itself is so small that it cannot be seen with the naked eye. The human body contains more than 50 trillion of them.

In the center of each cell, inside a special structure called the *nucleus,* can be found a group of extremely large molecules called *chromosomes.* These molecules direct the activity that goes on in the rest of the cell. They are made of deoxyribonucleic acid, a kind of nucleic acid usually referred to as *DNA*. The building blocks of DNA are small molecules called *nucleotides*. There are four different kinds of nucleotides that link together in a certain order to form the DNA molecule.

The order in which these molecules link together is very important. The purpose of the DNA molecule is to carry information concerning the working of the cell. This information is coded in the nucleotides. It is the order in which the nucleotides appear that makes up what we call the *genetic code*.

How does this code work? Well, we might compare the DNA molecule to a sentence of written words, such as the one you are reading now. The individual letters are like the atoms that make up the nucleotides. Those letters are put together into words, which might be thought of as small molecules, like the nucleotides themselves. These, in turn, are linked together to form sentences, paragraphs, even entire books. The DNA chromosomes, then, are like books, containing vast stores of information about how the cell works.

In fact, we might think of them as recipe books, because they contain recipes for making enzymes, the chemical machinery of the cell.

The DNA molecules also contain instructions for building cells. As your body grows, or as old cells die, new cells are needed to replace them. Sometimes your body simply needs new cells for special purposes. All of these cells are produced using the instructions in the DNA.

The first DNA molecule must have formed by accident in the primeval ocean. A chance combination of atoms must have produced a molecule that was capable of making crude copies of itself. It probably bore little resemblance to the DNA molecules that biologists study today.

Once this molecule had come into existence, however, it could have made limitless copies of itself, until the seas were filled with it. Not all of those copies would be identical. Sometimes, quite by accident, the duplicate molecule would be slightly different from the original. Such a mistake in copying is called a *mutation*.

Some of these mutations would actually be improvements over the original molecule. Eventually, a mutation might have arisen that could actually take control of its environment. This mutated molecule would have been able to manipulate the molecules around it in some way.

Remember, at this time the sea must have been full of organic molecules. After millions of years of mutation, our primitive DNA molecule must have learned to make its own enzymes out of these organic molecules. After another several million years, it might have built a protective shield around itself, using these molecules as building materials. This would have been the first cell—the distant ancestor of every cell in your body today.

Each cell in your body has a set of chromosomes in its nucleus that is identical to the chromosomes in every other cell in your body. These chromosomes, or rather the tiny structures they contain called *genes,* make you what you are. You received your chromosomes from your parents, some from your mother and some from your father. This is why you probably resemble your parents in some ways. You may have your father's nose and your mother's hair color, for example, or vice versa. (In some cases, you may have features that resemble neither of your parents'. This is because certain chromosomes have the ability to remain "silent" for one or more generations.)

All of this assumes that the chromosomes that you inherit are perfect copies of your parents' chromosomes. What if a mutation should occur? What if a chromosome has made a mistake in duplicating itself?

In this case, you would have some feature that does not come from anyone else. It would be a brand new feature, perhaps one that no human being has ever had before.

It has been estimated that as many as half the individuals alive today carry in their chromosomes at least one mutation, a genetic feature that did not exist before that generation. Most of these mutations, however, are minor. You could go through your entire life without being aware that you carried one.

This is probably for the best. The human body is a complex, finely tuned instrument. Any accidental genetic changes in its design are likely to be for the worse. The smaller the mutation, however, the less likely it is to do damage.

Yet over the centuries, small mutations can add up. If every other generation of a particular family imparts a new mutation to its offspring, after thousands of years there will be a noticeable change in the family's genetic makeup. Furthermore, as different families intermarry and exchange chromosomes, new mutations are added.

This makes chromosome duplication sound like a pretty sloppy process. How can a species of animal stay the same generation after generation if its chromosomes keep mutating?

The fact is, species not only can't stay the same, they don't. We can examine the remains, called *fossils,* of animals that lived millions of years ago. Some of these resemble animals that live today, but most are very different. None are exactly the same. The older the fossil, the more different it is from any animal living today. This would indicate that living creatures tend to change with time.

This tendency toward genetic change is called *evolution*.

When we examine the fossil remains of once-living creatures, we find that most of the changes that have occurred over the years have been for the better. Yet mutations are purely random. They happen by accident. As we saw a moment ago, they are usually harmful to the organism in which they occur. How can we explain this apparent contradiction?

While it is true that most mutations (perhaps 99.9 percent of them) are for the worse, every now and then a mutation occurs that is an improvement over the previous genetic design. The organism that inherits this mutation is actually better off than his or her relatives who did not. If there were some process that sifted out the good mutations from the bad, it would explain this steady improvement of the species.

There is such a process. It was revealed in 1859, when the famous naturalist Charles Darwin published his book, *The Origin of Species*. Darwin called the process *natural selection*.

Some years before, Darwin had read the work of the English philosopher Thomas Malthus. Malthus had speculated that living organisms tended to multiply faster than the resources of the earth could support them; in other words, there would never be enough food, shelter, or other necessities to go around. For this reason, a large percentage of the organisms born in any given year would die before living out their natural life spans. More importantly, they would die before they were mature enough to have offspring of their own—and pass their chromosomes on to the next generation.

Darwin, upon reading this, asked himself an important question: Which organisms would tend to die and which would tend to survive? The answer was deceptively simple. The organisms that survived would be those that were best at surviving.

This is the basic principle of natural selection. Some organisms will inherit mutations that will make them better at surviving. Other organisms will inherit mutations that will make them less likely to survive. As all of these organisms scramble for survival in a world of limited resources, the ones that inherit "good" mutations will tend to survive while the ones that inherit "bad" mutations will tend to die young, before being able to pass its chromosomes on to the next generation.

Given enough time, is there any limit to changes an organism can go through?

No one can say. However, earlier we saw how the primeval ocean produced one-celled organisms that floated in the water and fed on sunlight and organic molecules. These one-celled organisms multiplied by duplicating their DNA, the same way the cells in your body divide today. The moment the first DNA molecules began dividing in the primeval ocean, the process of natural selection went into action. Every mutation in the primitive DNA was sifted by this process for its survival value. Good mutations survived. Bad mutations died.

In this way, more and more complicated organisms appeared. Some cells acquired the ability to make their own food through the process of photosynthesis. They stored the sun's energy as molecules of simple sugars. Other cells adapted to eating these cells, using the sugar molecules as food and liberating the stored energy inside their own bodies.

We saw at the beginning of the chapter that there was no oxygen in the primitive atmosphere. This is not entirely true. There were oxygen atoms, but these were trapped inside molecules, where they were linked to other kinds of atoms. When photosynthesis began breaking up the molecules in the air, the oxygen atoms were released. Atoms of oxygen that are not linked to other kinds of atoms are called *free oxygen.*

Oxygen atoms are very quick to combine with other kinds of atoms. If there had been free oxygen in the air when the first organic molecules were forming, the oxygen atoms would have disrupted the process, and life could not have formed.

Once photosynthesis had begun, however, free oxygen began to build up in the atmosphere. It was this oxygen that allowed more complicated forms of life to evolve—including human beings.

The first living organisms lived in the water. In fact, until less than a billion years ago, all life was in the sea. The radiation from the sun was too intense for living creatures to survive on the land. Only the depths of the sea offered enough protection. But as photosynthesis gradually released free oxygen into the

*The fossil of a once-living
sea creature, preserved in rock.*

atmosphere, a protective shell of gases came to surround our planet. This screened out the most dangerous radiations. Once the land was safe for living creatures, organisms evolved that could live on its surface. First came plants, then insects.

By this time, about 3.5 billion years had passed since the first living molecules had formed. Evolution still went on as it had in the beginning. Chromosomes made mistakes in copying themselves, and sometimes these mistakes were better than the original. In this way, new plants and animals were constantly coming into existence.

Somewhere on this earth half a billion years ago, a distant ancestor of the human race was born, a fish probably, though not quite like any fish we know of today. It must have resembled what we now call a lungfish, a fish that is able to live out of water for long periods of time.

There were many advantages to this. In times of drought, when the water dried up and the fish found itself on land, it could burrow into the mud and wait for rain. Or it could use its fins to drag itself to the nearest pool of water. Those fins must have evolved into legs, the gills into lungs. Such a fish would eventually have evolved into a creature that could live both in water and out of it—an *amphibian.* Modern amphibians include frogs, toads, and salamanders.

From the amphibians evolved the *reptiles.* For more than a hundred million years these reptiles ruled the earth. Huge reptiles called dinosaurs thrived in many different settings—on land, in the sea, and in the air.

The reptiles, however, were cold-blooded. That is, the temperature of their bodies changed according to the temperature around them. In cold weather, these reptiles would become sluggish, slow-moving. At first, this didn't matter very much. In those days, the temperature over most of the earth was pretty much the same. Temperatures in winter were not all that different from temperatures in summer. In time, however, these differences became greater, perhaps even greater than they are today. Warm-blooded creatures began to evolve. These are animals with body temperatures that do not change with the weather. In the struggle for survival, warm-blooded creatures now had the advantage. They did not become sluggish when the weather turned cold. They could feed off the eggs of the cold-blooded dinosaurs. And the dinosaurs, made slow-moving by the cold weather, would be unable to stop them.

These warm-blooded creatures were the *birds* and *mammals*. The birds, it is now believed, are direct descendants of the dinosaurs. The mammals (including humans) descended from other sorts of reptiles.

Today, only a few reptiles survive—alligators and turtles, for instance. Birds and mammals, on the other hand, are among the most common creatures on earth.

Human beings are mammals belonging to a specific order of mammal called the *primates.* Other primates include monkeys and apes. The first primates evolved about 60 million years ago.

Early primates lived mostly in the trees. Life in the treetops called for quick thinking, good vision, and physical coordination. Without these qualities, a tree-dwelling animal might not grasp a limb the right way. It might then plummet to its death on the ground below.

Because of this, primates developed large brains and superior eyesight. In a sense, humans owe their intelligence and visual ability to the fact that their ancestors lived in trees.

One of the things that sets humans apart from other primates is our use of tools. We are able to use natural objects—stones, tree limbs, bones—in such a way that we can control our environment. We can use these objects as weapons, for instance, or for digging or hammering. We are also able to make tools of our own—arrows or levers or screwdrivers or wheels. Some scientists suggest that tools made us what we are today. Once tools had been invented, having the intelli-

Lizards are one of the relatively few remaining members of the reptile family. The great dinosaurs that once ruled the earth were reptiles.

Today, it is mammals,
such as primates and marsupials,
that dominate the earth.

gence to use them became important to our survival. As humans became more intelligent, we made better tools. As we made better tools, we became even more intelligent, the better to use those tools, and so on.

And so life came to dominate the face of the earth. Air, water, rock, and now life—those are the things that make the earth what it is. The things that make the earth . . . unique.

Civilization may have begun in the Nile delta. Here we see jet stream clouds crossing above the Nile River and Egypt.

CHAPTER SEVEN

THE LIVING EARTH

The green of grass and leaves, the brown of tree bark, the varied hues of flowers and flesh—these are the colors we think of when we think of the earth. These and the blue of the sea and sky, the amber shades of the desert, the white of snow.

Life changes the shape of the earth as surely as do the wind and rain. It covers the earth with a soft carpet, sending its roots down into the soil and even into the rock. It changes the air that it breathes, alters the molecules of the water it drinks.

In fact, every element that makes up our world affects every other element. It is impossible to study any one of these elements in isolation, without looking at the others. Air, water, rock, and life—each shapes the other, each changes the other, in a constant, unending cycle. Touch one, and you touch them all.

Over billions of years life has adapted with great precision to its natural environment. The living organisms that make up the so-called *biosphere* ("sphere of life") of our planet work together as though they were a single, vast organism. In fact, the earth itself can be looked at as a single organism, with all of its parts, living and nonliving, working together just as the organs in your body work together. The study of this giant organism, and the relationship of its parts, is called *ecology*. The relationship itself is called the *ecological balance*.

The earth's ecological balance is a complex thing, and it did not come about by accident.

We have seen that evolution is a question of survival. Those organisms best equipped to survive live to pass on their chromosomes. If, as Malthus stated, there are more living creatures born on this planet than the earth is capable of supporting, then there must be competition between these creatures.

Suppose that two different species of animal live on the same kind of food—a certain variety of nuts, for instance. Because the nut will exist only in limited quantity, there may not be enough to go around. It follows that there will be intense competition between the two species in gathering the nuts. As natural selection and mutation bestow these animals with better methods of obtaining the nuts, one species will eventually become more skilled at nut-gathering than the other. The loser at this competition—the species that did not adapt quickly enough to keep up—will find itself facing possible starvation.

Unless it can learn to eat some other kind of food.

In this way, every species finds its *ecological niche,* the particular manner in which it is best at surviving. Some creatures adapt to eating other creatures; this is their niche. Other creatures adapt so as not to be eaten. These are some of the ways in which the ecological balance is created.

If a species of animal is poor at gathering food, either it will get better or starve, especially if it is forced to compete with other animals for its niche. On the other hand, if a species is *too* good at gathering food, it faces another peril—it may destroy its own niche. Suppose, for instance, that a species of frog has adapted to eating flies. If it is too good at finding flies, the flies may disappear, become *extinct.* Then there will be no more food for the frogs. Unless they can change their dietary habits, the frogs, too, will become extinct.

Of course, as the frogs become better at eating flies, the flies in turn become better at not getting eaten. If the flies become too good at eluding the frogs, the frogs may die of starvation—and the fly population will expand out of control, without the frogs to hold their numbers down. If the flies carry disease, as do certain insects in tropical areas, this could pose a danger to other animal populations, including humans.

The ecological balance is a very delicate thing.

You might guess from what we just said that adaptability has a very high survival value. A species that can adapt to a new ecological niche when necessary is more likely to survive than a species that cannot. The more specialized a species becomes—that is, the narrower its ecological niche—the more likely it is to become extinct. Under most circumstances, specialization has a fairly low survival value. Adaptability has a high survival value.

Human beings are among the least specialized creatures on earth, and the most adaptable. We occupy an extremely broad ecological niche. We can live in a wide variety of environments and eat a wide variety of foods.

It is tempting to suggest human beings are the most successful product of the earth's biosphere, a shining example of what evolution can produce. But we have competition for this title. Insects, for instance, far outnumber human beings, as do bacteria. The lowly cockroach has survived many times longer than humanity has.

Furthermore, there is some evidence that humans have become too good at exploiting their ecological niche. Human hunters have wiped out entire species of animals. We have destroyed the habitats of living creatures, through the construction of buildings, highways, and dams, and the testing of bombs.

This is no small thing. The extinction of a single species of animal reverberates throughout the entire ecology like an explosion. The extinction of our imaginary species of frog, for instance, could unleash on humanity a horde of disease-ridden flies. When large populations of rats have been killed, for instance, the fleas that lived on those rats began to infest other animals, including humans. And such fleas have carried diseases as deadly as the bubonic plague.

The ecological balance is a delicate thing.

Human activity affects not only the biosphere but the atmosphere as well. Factories, belching forth clouds of smoke, fill the air with carbon dioxide. As the amount of carbon dioxide in the atmosphere increases, heat from the sun becomes trapped, producing a greenhouse effect (see chapter two). A worldwide temperature increase averaging only a few degrees could begin to melt the polar ice caps. The coastal areas of all the continents would be flooded. Millions of lives would be lost.

In previous chapters we saw how the face of the earth is altered by wind and rain, and by life itself. Yet perhaps human beings are the greatest force for change on this planet. We hold in our hands the ability to reshape our world.

And yet we still have so much to learn. One day, perhaps, we will control the weather, the flow of the sea, the very shape of the continents. We will control these things because we will understand the ways in which they can be controlled.

Today, however, we have only a very limited amount of knowledge. If we use this knowledge carelessly, we could well destroy the planet that we live on, or render it uninhabitable.

The earth is the only world we know of where life has come into existence. Most likely, it is the only such world in the solar system. For all we know, it is the only such world in the universe, though this is less likely. Still, the odds against life appearing on any given world must be very large. Planets like the earth must be very rare.

If our solar system is ever visited by intelligent beings from another world, ours is almost certainly the planet they will be interested in. Not beautiful Saturn, not majestic Jupiter, not hot and tiny little Mercury or distant and cold Pluto or hellish

Venus. There must be billions of planets like these, scattered throughout the universe.

No, the planet they will want to visit will certainly be the earth, home of lush vegetation and diverse wildlife—and intelligent beings.

But will these beings from other worlds greet us as the fellow miracles that we are, living examples of the universe's capacity to create wonderful things? Or will they simply explore the ruins that we leave behind, the relics of a race that destroyed its ecological niche because it did not fully understand the world on which it lived?

Planet Earth is at a turning point right now. Its future—and the future of the human race—hangs in the balance. There are many ways that we can destroy ourselves: pollution, nuclear war, famine, disease, breakdown of the ecological balance. It is in our power to prevent these disasters and perhaps even make the earth a better place for all living creatures. But to do so we must first understand this world that we call the earth, how its parts fit together, and how we fit into the whole.

The earth's future is our future as well.

GLOSSARY

Abyssal plain—the flat, basaltic ocean bottom, beyond the continental shelf.

Air mass—large segment of air, of about the same temperature and pressure throughout.

Archipelago—a group of islands.

Atmosphere—the shell of air surrounding a planet; on earth the atmosphere is mostly nitrogen and oxygen.

Atoms—the basic units of matter.

Biosphere—the part of the earth on which organisms can live.

Cell—the unit from which all living creatures, plants and animals, are constructed. The human body is made up of several trillion cells, each one containing the basic machinery that keeps us alive.

Chromosomes—large, complex molecules that contain the genes on which are recorded the information that makes us what we are.

Continental shelf—the submerged portion of the continental land mass that slants gradually down toward the abyssal plain.

Core—the innermost section of the earth. Actually, there are two cores, one inside the other. The *inner core* is solid while the *outer core* is liquid.

Crest—the highest part of a wave.

Crust—the outermost portion of the earth; the thin shell of solid rocky materials that lies on top of the mantle.

Earthquake—a sudden, sometimes destructive movement of the earth's surface caused by pressures building up within the earth.

Ecological niche—the way in which a particular organism in the biosphere interacts with other organisms and with the environment.

Ecology—the study of the ways in which living and nonliving entities interact within an environment.

Erosion—the gradual (and sometimes not so gradual) wearing away of rocks and other elements of the earth's surface under the action of wind, rain, temperature changes, and other environmental forces.

Evolution—the way in which living creatures change slowly with time.

Extinct—an adjective referring to a species of organism that has died out completely.

Fetch—the distance over which the wind blows.

Fossils—remains of once-living organisms, usually preserved underground in the form of bones or petrified flesh.

Front—the point at which two air masses meet. Often the scene of violent storm activity.

Glaciers—great fields of ice formed when snow accumulates faster than it can melt.

Gravity—the force of attraction, common to all matter; gravity prevents us from simply leaping off into space. It also keeps the planets in motion around the sun.

Greenhouse effect—occurs when more heat enters the atmosphere of a planet than leaves it; the buildup of heat that results is called the greenhouse effect because it resembles the way in which heat builds up in a greenhouse.

Hydrogen fusion—the violent collision of two hydrogen atoms resulting in the formation of a single helium atom; a way of releasing energy from within the atom.

Ice age—a period during which temperatures become unusually low in normally temperate regions. Glaciers often form.

Igneous rock—rock formed by the heating and melting of older rocks.

Magma—extremely hot molten or plastic rock within the earth.

Mantle—the portion of the earth that lies beneath the crust. Rocks within the mantle are extremely hot, but are kept in a plastic (semisolid or semiliquid) state by the pressure of the rocks above.

Metamorphic rock—rocks formed within the earth when older rocks are put under intense pressures.

Mutation—a sudden change in an organism's genes. Mutations are responsible for evolution, along with natural selection.

Natural selection—when mutations occur in an organism's genes, some of these changes are for the better and some are for the worse. (*Most* are for the worse.) Those organisms with mutations for the worse usually die off, while those with mutations for the better survive. Because the good mutations are *selected*, this process is called natural selection.

Organic molecules—large chains of atoms that occur almost exclusively in living organisms. The chromosomes, for instance, are organic molecules.

Outgassing—the release of gas from within rocks by volcanic action. Outgassing supplied the primitive earth with its atmosphere.

Plate tectonics—the motion of the "plates" that make up the earth's surface. Sometimes called *continental drift*.

Protein—a kind of organic molecule found in all living cells; made up of a chain of smaller molecules called *amino acids*.

Radiation—a form of energy that radiates ("moves outward in all directions") from a source. Light is a form of radiation, as are radio waves, X rays, etc.

Sedimentary rock—rock formed from the accumulation of fragments of old rocks, the bodies of tiny organisms, and other bits of matter. Usually formed at the bottom of rivers, where these particles settle downward as *sediment.*

Storm surge—a giant wave formed by the piling up of smaller waves during a very strong wind.

Subduction zone—the area in which one plate of the earth's surface sinks beneath another, usually found underwater at the edge of continents. Often the site of submerged trenches.

Tide—the rising and falling of the ocean waters, usually occurring twice a day and caused mostly by the gravity of the moon.

Trench—an extremely deep area of the ocean bottom, usually found at or near subduction zones.

Trough—the lowest part of a wave.

Tsunami—a giant wave usually formed by underwater earthquakes or volcanoes.

Weather—the behavior of the earth's atmosphere, caused largely by the heat of the sun.

FOR FURTHER READING

Ames, Gerald and Rose Wyler. *The Earth's Story*. New York: Creative Educational Society, 1962.

Asimov, Isaac. *How Did We Find Out About Volcanoes?* New York: Walker & Co., 1981.

Berger, Melvin. *Disastrous Volcanoes*. New York: Franklin Watts, Inc., 1981.

Gallant, Roy A. *Exploring Under the Earth*. New York: Garden City Books, 1960.

Heintze, Carl. *The Circle of Fire*. New York: Meredith Press, 1968.

Kiefer, Irene. *Global Jigsaw Puzzle: The Story of Continental Drift*. New York: Atheneum, 1978.

INDEX